faith

STRENGTHENING YOUR
RELATIONSHIP WITH GOD

SKINNY BROWN DOG
MEDIA
EST. 2013
ATLANTA | PUNTA DEL ESTE

Published by Skinny Brown Dog Media
Atlanta, GA /Punta del Este, Uruguay

For Information, Contact:
Distributed by Skinny Brown Dog Media
SkinnyBrownDogMedia.com
Email: Info@SkinnyBrownDogMedia.com

Faith
Strengthening Your Relationship with God
Whole Life Devotional Series
By Eric G Reid

Library of Congress Catalog in Publication Data
ISBN eBook   978 1 965235 25 6
ISBN trade paperback   978 1 965235 22 5
ISBN Hardback Dust Jacketed   978 1 965235 23 2
ISBN case laminate   978 1 965235 24 9

CONTENTS

WEEK 1
Laying the Foundation of Faith

WEEK 2
Deepening Your Faith

WEEK 3
Living Out Faith in Daily Life

DEDICATION

To those who lifted me when I felt weakest and my faith seemed lost,
Your unwavering support, fellowship, friendship, and grace
carried me through some dark days.
Thank you for walking this journey with me.

"For where two or three gather in my name, there am I with them."
—Matthew 18:20

Faith

Ever heard those incredible stories of faith that sound almost like superhero tales? You know, the ones where someone lifts a car to save a child or feeds a crowd with just a few loaves and fish. If you're like me, you might think, "Wow, that's amazing... but there's no way I could do that." I remember feeling that way when I first heard about George Müller, who ran orphanages on faith alone, or Brother Andrew, who smuggled Bibles into closed countries.

Well, here's the thing: that kind of faith isn't some exclusive club for spiritual superheroes. It's available to all of us, and it starts with small, everyday steps to grow closer to God. Trust me, I'm no superhero, but I've seen God work in amazing ways when I've taken those small steps of faith.

Welcome to "Faith: Strengthening Your Relationship with God," part of the Whole Life Devotional Series. This book is all about helping you build a vibrant, everyday faith that can transform your life in real, tangible ways. Whether you're just starting out on your faith journey or you've been walking with God for years, there's always room to grow.

Faith isn't just one piece of our spiritual puzzle; it's the foundation everything else sits on. Without it, we can't please God Hebrews 11:6 tells us that. It's what anchors us when life gets stormy and gives us hope and direction. Through faith, we experience the fullness of God's love and power. I've seen this play out in my own life, and let me tell you, it's a gamechanger.

In this book, we're going to explore what it really means to live a life of faith. We'll look at how to nurture and grow our faith, just like a plant needs water, sunlight, and good soil to thrive. I'll share some tools and practices that have helped me strengthen my faith and deepen my relationship with God. And don't worry, we'll take it step by step.

We're in this together for a threeweek journey. Each week, we'll focus on a different aspect of faith, guiding you stepbystep in building a solid foundation, growing your faith, and living it out in practical ways. Through daily scripture readings, reflections, and actionable steps, you'll be encouraged and challenged to go deeper in your faith walk. And who knows? You might just surprise yourself with what God can do through you.

Ready to get started? Let's dive in and see how God can work in our lives when we take those small steps of faith. Trust me, it's an adventure worth taking.

Why This Study?

In today's fastpaced and everchanging world, many of us struggle with questions of faith. We are constantly bombarded with messages from the media, society, and even our own social circles about what we should believe and how we should live. These worldly influences can often lead us away from a true and vibrant faith, creating confusion, doubt, and a sense of spiritual dryness.

This study is designed to help you cut through the noise and focus on what truly matters: your relationship with God. By dedicating time each day to study the Bible, pray, and reflect, you will be able to cultivate a deeper and more resilient faith. This devotional is not just about gaining knowledge; it is about transformation. It's about allowing God's Word to penetrate your heart and change your life.

In a world that values instant gratification and superficial connections, developing a meaningful and enduring faith can seem daunting. Many of us find ourselves drifting, feeling spiritually dry and disconnected. This study aims to address these challenges by providing a structured approach to deepening your faith. Through consistent engagement with scripture, prayer, and reflection, you will be equipped to navigate the complexities of modern life with a faith that is both steadfast and dynamic.

Furthermore, this devotional encourages a personal journey that goes beyond surfacelevel understanding. It invites you to explore the depths of your relationship with God, uncovering the richness of His promises and the strength found in His presence. By immersing yourself in this study, you will discover practical ways to integrate your faith into everyday life, making it a living and active part of who you are.

This study also emphasizes the importance of community. While personal reflection is crucial, sharing your journey with others can provide additional support, encouragement, and accountability. Engaging with fellow believers can enhance your understanding and application of faith, fostering a sense of belonging and mutual growth.

Ultimately, this study is about transformation. It's about moving from a place of uncertainty and spiritual dryness to a vibrant, faith filled life. By committing to this journey, you are opening yourself up to the transformative power of God's Word. You will learn to trust Him more deeply, love Him more fully, and live out your faith more authentically.

In short, this study provides a comprehensive approach to strengthening your relationship with God. It offers tools and insights to help you navigate the noise of the world, deepen your faith, and experience true spiritual growth. As you embark on this journey, be prepared for a transformation that will touch every aspect of your life, bringing you closer to the vibrant and resilient faith you desire.

The Importance of Faith

Your faith shapes how you see yourself, how you interact with others, and how you navigate the world. When your faith is rooted in God, it provides a solid foundation that stands firm amidst the shifting sands of life. I once thought having faith was like having an invisible safety net. Turns out, it's more like having a rocksolid fortress. A strong faith brings clarity, purpose, and a deep sense of belonging. It allows you to live confidently, knowing that you are loved and valued by the Creator of the universe.

In contrast, when your faith is influenced by worldly standards and expectations, it can lead to instability and a lack of fulfillment. Take it from someone who tried living by the world's standards and found it exhausting. Worldly faith is often based on external factors such as circumstances, feelings, and achievements. These factors are transient and can change rapidly, leaving you feeling uncertain and insecure. By grounding your faith in God, you can experience a sense of peace and stability that transcends the ups and downs of life.

When I first started my journey of faith, I thought it would be like flipping a switch and suddenly having everything figured out. Spoiler alert: it's more like a lifelong renovation project with God as the master builder. And trust me, His plans are way better than any DIY project I could come up with. Faith is not a onetime decision but an ongoing commitment to trust in God's plan, even when things don't make sense.

Faith vs. Hope

It's important to distinguish between faith and hope, as they are closely related but not identical. Faith is the assurance of things hoped for, the conviction of things not seen Hebrews 11:1. It is a deepseated trust in God and His promises, regardless of our current circumstances. Faith says, "I believe that God is who He says He is and will do what He says He will do."

Hope, on the other hand, is the confident expectation and desire for a certain thing to happen. It is forwardlooking and often tied to specific outcomes or desires. While faith provides the foundation, hope builds upon it, giving us the strength to look towards the future with optimism and assurance. Hope says, "I eagerly anticipate the good things that God has in store for me."

Faith and hope work together in our spiritual journey. Faith grounds us in the present, giving us the strength to face today's challenges with trust and confidence in God. Hope propels us forward, encouraging us to look to the future with a positive and expectant heart. Both are essential for a vibrant and resilient spiritual life.

When I struggled with uncertainty, it was my faith that kept me anchored, and my hope that kept me moving forward. Together, they create a powerful dynamic that allows us to live with peace and joy, knowing that God is in control of both our present and our future.

In summary, faith and hope are intertwined in our walk with God. Faith provides the solid foundation upon which hope builds. By nurturing both, we can navigate life's challenges with confidence, trust, and a forwardlooking perspective that keeps us anchored in God's promises and open to His plans for our lives.

What Can Be Gained?

Engaging with this study offers numerous benefits:

- Clarity and Confidence: By understanding your faith in Christ, you will gain clarity about your purpose and direction in life. This newfound clarity will empower you to make decisions confidently and live with a sense of intentionality and purpose. Imagine waking up each day with a clear sense of direction— kind of like having a builtin GPS for your soul.

- Spiritual Growth: Daily engagement with scripture and reflective questions will deepen your relationship with God. As you spend time in prayer and meditation, you will become more attuned to His voice and guidance. Picture your faith as a plant that needs daily watering and sunlight. With consistent care, it will grow strong and flourish.

- Resilience Against Worldly Pressures: By recognizing and resisting the influences of worldly faith, you will develop resilience. This will help you stand firm in your faith, even when faced with challenges and temptations. It's like building spiritual muscles that help you lift the heavy weights of life's pressures.

- Authentic Community: Understanding the importance of community and support in your spiritual journey will encourage you to build and maintain meaningful relationships with fellow believers. These connections will provide encouragement, accountability, and a sense of belonging. Think of it as having a faith family that's always got your back.

- Practical Application: Each day's action plan provides practical steps to apply what you've learned, making the principles of a godly faith a tangible part of your daily life. This will help you integrate your faith into every aspect of your existence. It's like turning your faith from theory into practice, one step at a time.

- Inner Peace and Joy: Discovering and living out your true faith in God brings a profound sense of peace and joy. You will experience the contentment that comes from knowing you are loved and valued by your Creator and that your life has a meaningful purpose. It's that deep, abiding joy that sticks with you even on the tough days.

So as we embark on this journey, let's do it with open hearts and a willingness to grow. Expect challenges, but also expect incredible growth and transformation. Together, we'll navigate the highs and lows, always grounded in the unshakable foundation of our faith in God.

Journey of Faith Transformation

This study is not just about gaining knowledge; it is about transformation. If you're like me, you might have started this journey thinking you already knew a thing or two about faith. I remember thinking, "I've got this!" only to realize I had a lot to learn. The beauty of faith is that it's a journey, not a destination, and there's always room to grow.

As you work through each day's readings and reflections, allow the Holy Spirit to work in your heart and mind. Be open to the changes that God wants to make in your life. Sometimes those changes are subtle, like a gentle nudge, and other times they're more like a divine twobyfour. Either way, embrace the process of becoming who He has created you to be. Trust me, the journey is worth it.

Transformation requires intentionality. It involves making a conscious effort to align your thoughts, attitudes, and actions with

God's truth. I've had my fair share of moments where I've had to check myself and ask, "Is this what God wants for me, or am I just doing my own thing?" Spoiler alert: Doing things God's way always turns out better. This study will guide you through this process, providing the tools and support you need to grow and mature in your faith.

And let's be honest, there will be times when you stumble. We all do. Like the time I confidently volunteered to lead a prayer group and realized halfway through that I had no idea what I was doing. It was humbling, to say the least. But those moments are part of the transformation too. They teach us humility, reliance on God, and the importance of community.

Now, it's important to note that this devotional is not designed to be a deep dive into theological studies. Instead, it is a practical guide to building the habit of spending 15 minutes a day in devotional time. Think of it as planting seeds of faith that, with consistent care, will grow into a strong and flourishing relationship with God.

Let me share a story that illustrates this concept perfectly. When I first started gardening, I was eager to see immediate results. I planted a whole garden in one day, expecting a lush, green oasis by the next week. Spoiler alert: It didn't work out that way. The plants struggled, and so did I. It wasn't until I committed to small, daily tasks—watering, weeding, and nurturing the plants—that I saw real growth. Over time, those small efforts led to a thriving garden. Similarly, our faith grows through small, consistent actions rather than grand, sporadic gestures.

So buckle up for this journey of faith transformation. Expect to be challenged, expect to grow, and expect to see God move in your life in ways you never imagined. Remember, it's not about perfection; it's about progress. And with each step, you're becoming more of the person God created you to be.

Let's embrace this journey together with open hearts and a willingness to be transformed. God has incredible plans for you, and as you lean into this study, you'll find yourself drawn closer to Him and more in tune with His will for your life. So take a deep breath, grab your Bible, and let's get started. The journey of transformation awaits!

How to Use This Devotional

Each day of this devotional is structured to provide a holistic approach to understanding and embracing your faith in God. Here's how to make the most of it:

1. Scripture Readings: Begin each day by reading the suggested scriptures. Take your time to read and reflect on the passages, allowing God's Word to speak to your heart. Think of this as your spiritual breakfast—fuel to start your day right.
2. Devotional Thought: Read the devotional thought for the day. These reflections are designed to help you understand and apply the scriptures to your life. Spend time journaling about what you've read and how it resonates with you. Use the journal prompts to guide your reflections and capture your thoughts and feelings. Consider this your personal chat with God where you get to process and personalize His message.
3. Questions for Reflection: Spend time pondering the reflection questions. These questions are meant to provoke deep thought and personal application. Consider journaling your responses to capture your insights and growth. This is your opportunity to dig deep and uncover the layers of your faith journey.
4. Daily Action Plan: Each day includes a practical action step to help you live out the principles you've learned. These actions will

reinforce your understanding and encourage you to integrate godly faith into your daily life. Think of these steps as your faith in action—little changes that lead to big transformations.

5. Prayer: End each day with a time of prayer. Ask God to help you embrace your faith in Him and to guide you in living out His purpose for your life. This is your chance to connect deeply with God, laying down your worries and seeking His guidance.

Remember, this devotional is for you and you alone. If a day takes a week, relax—it's okay. The gift of this time of reading, reflection, and prayer is that it's meant to meet you where you are, at your own pace. There's no rush; the journey of faith is a lifelong adventure. Enjoy the process and give yourself the grace to move through it as needed.

By following this structure, you will be able to deepen your faith and strengthen your relationship with God. Each part of this devotional is designed to build upon the other, creating a comprehensive and transformative experience. So grab your Bible, your journal, and let's dive in together. This journey is about growth, discovery, and becoming who God has called you to be.

WEEK 1
Laying the Foundation of Faith

Welcome to Week 1 of our devotional journey, where we will focus on laying a solid foundation of faith. Just like building a house, you need a strong foundation to support everything else. Our faith acts as this foundation, anchoring us through life's storms and helping us grow into the people God created us to be.

During this week, we will explore what it means to have a firm foundation in faith. We'll dive into the basics of what faith is, how it functions in our lives, and why it's essential for our spiritual growth. Think of this as setting the groundwork for everything that follows. Without a solid foundation, even the most beautiful structure will crumble under pressure.

We'll also examine how faith influences our daily decisions, our relationships, and our overall perspective on life. Whether you're new to your faith journey or have been walking with God for years, reinforcing your foundation is crucial. It's a chance to revisit the core of your beliefs, to strengthen what you already know, and to discover new dimensions of your faith.

Let's get ready to dig deep, ask questions, and open our hearts to the transformative power of faith. As we lay this foundation together, we can build a stronger, more resilient spiritual life that stands the test of time.

Key Themes

- Understanding Faith: Grasping what faith truly means and how it impacts our daily lives.
- Trusting God's Promises: Learning to rely on God's promises even when we can't see the outcome.

- Daily Spiritual Practices: Developing consistent habits that nurture and strengthen our faith.

Anchor Scripture

"Now faith is confidence in what we hope for and assurance about what we do not see."
—Hebrews 11:1

This verse from Hebrews sets the tone for our week. Faith isn't about having all the answers; it's about trusting in God's promises and having confidence in what we hope for, even when we can't see it.

Questions for Reflection

1. What does faith mean to you personally?

_____

_____

_____

2. How has your understanding of faith evolved over time?

_____

_____

_____

3. In what areas of your life do you find it hardest to have faith?

_____

_____

_____

Building Deeper Connection to Faith

- Journaling Prompt: Reflect on moments when your faith was challenged. How did you respond, and what did you learn?
- Suggested Prayer: "Heavenly Father, help me to build a strong foundation of faith. Teach me to trust in Your promises and to seek Your guidance in every aspect of my life. Amen."

Tomorrow's Journey

This week, we will lay the groundwork for a faith that stands strong and tall, no matter what life throws our way. Each day will bring new insights and opportunities to deepen your faith. Let's embark on this journey together with open hearts and minds.

DAY 1
WHAT IS FAITH?

Let's start with a little story from my own life. When I was a kid, I had this brilliant idea to build a treehouse. I envisioned it as a grand fortress in the sky, where I'd rule my imaginary kingdom. Armed with some planks of wood and a hammer, I got to work. My enthusiasm was skyhigh, but my construction skills? Not so much. The treehouse ended up being more of a precarious platform than a sturdy fortress.

Looking back, I realize this experience taught me something profound about faith. Just like my treehouse needed a strong base to stand tall, I've found that my faith needs a solid foundation to weather life's storms. There have been times when my faith felt as shaky as that treehouse platform, moments when I questioned and doubted. But I've also experienced times when my faith stood firm, giving me strength I didn't know I had.

For me, faith isn't just about believing in something unseen. It's a deep, personal trust that has grown through both joyful and challenging times. It's the feeling I get when I pray and sense a presence greater than myself. It's the peace I find when I'm overwhelmed and remember that I'm not alone. Faith, I've discovered, is less about having all the answers and more about trusting the journey, even when the path ahead is unclear.

Role Models in Scripture

Consider the life of David, the shepherd boy who became king. David's journey is one of the most remarkable transformations in the Bible. He started as the youngest son of Jesse, tending sheep in the fields. He was so unremarkable in the eyes of his family that when the prophet Samuel came to anoint the next king of Israel, David wasn't even initially considered. But God saw something different. God saw David's heart.

One day, David was sent to deliver food to his brothers on the battlefield. It was there that he heard the giant Goliath taunting the Israelites and defying God. While the entire Israelite army trembled in fear, David, fueled by his unwavering faith in God, stepped forward. Despite his youth and lack of military experience, he declared, "*The Lord who rescued me from the paw of the lion and the paw of the bear will rescue me from the hand of this Philistine*" 1 Samuel 17:37.

David's faith wasn't based on his own strength or abilities. It was rooted in his trust in God's power and faithfulness. He remembered how God had delivered him from past dangers and believed that God would do it again. David's story reminds us that our faith should be grounded in God's character and promises, not in our circumstances or abilities.

When David faced Goliath, he didn't see an insurmountable obstacle; he saw an opportunity for God to demonstrate His power and faithfulness. His faith gave him the courage to step forward when others were paralyzed by fear. And God honored that faith, giving David the victory and establishing him as a key figure in Israel's history.

Just like David, we are called to have a faith that looks beyond the giants in our lives and sees the greatness of our God. It's a faith that trusts in God's ability to deliver and provide, even when the odds seem stacked against us.

Scripture to Remember

"Now faith is the assurance of things hoped for, the conviction of things not seen."
—Hebrews 11:1

"The Lord who rescued me from the paw of the lion and the paw of the bear will rescue me from the hand of this Philistine."
—1 Samuel 17:37

"Trust in the Lord with all your heart and lean not on your own understanding; in all your ways submit to Him, and He will make your paths straight."
—Proverbs 3:56

Consider This

Reflect on the significance of having a solid foundation of faith. Think about how David's faith in God gave him the courage to face Goliath. Spend time journaling about areas in your life where you need to trust God more deeply.

Questions for Reflection

1. How does David's story challenge your understanding of faith?

_____

_____

_____

2. What "giants" are you facing in your life that require you to trust God?

_____

_____

_____

3. How can you build a stronger foundation of faith in your daily life?

_____

_____

_____

Living Out Our Faith

Identify one area of your life where you need to strengthen your faith. Write it down and pray, asking God to help you trust Him more deeply in this area. Commit to taking one practical step this week to build your faith.

_____

_____

_____

_____

_____

_____

Building Deeper Connection to Faith

- Journaling Prompt: Reflect on a time when you trusted God in a challenging situation. How did this experience shape your faith?

- Suggested Prayer: "Lord, help me to build a strong foundation of faith. Teach me to trust in Your promises and rely on Your strength. Give me the courage to face the giants in my life, knowing that You are with me. Amen."

Tomorrow's Journey

Today, we've laid the first stone in the foundation of our faith by understanding what faith is and how it can empower us to face life's challenges. Tomorrow, we will delve deeper into the relationship between faith and doubt.

DAY 2
FAITH AND DOUBT

When I was learning to ride a bike, I remember vividly the mix of excitement and fear. The first few attempts were wobbly, and I crashed more times than I care to admit. My big sister, my hero and role model on so many things, would encourage me, saying, "You can do it! Just keep pedaling!" But every time I fell, doubt would creep in, making me question if I'd ever manage to ride without training wheels. That same doubt and fear often accompany our faith journey. Just like learning to ride a bike, our faith journey is filled with moments of uncertainty and fear. We start off with enthusiasm, but when we encounter obstacles or fall down, doubt can quickly take over.

Doubt is a natural part of the faith journey. It's something we all experience at one time or another. But it's also through doubt that we can seek and find deeper understanding and trust in God. Just like I had to keep pedaling despite my falls, we must keep moving forward in our faith, even when doubts arise. Trusting God means believing that He will catch us when we stumble and guide us back on track.

Role Models in Scripture

Let's dive into one of the most captivating moments in Peter's life, a story that beautifully encapsulates the tension between faith and doubt. Picture this: it's the dead of night, and the disciples are out on a boat, battling fierce waves and howling winds. They're exhausted, probably wondering why Jesus sent them ahead while He stayed behind to pray.

Then, out of nowhere, they see a figure walking on the water. Imagine the scene: grown men, seasoned fishermen, absolutely terrified. They think they're seeing a ghost. But amidst their fear, a familiar voice calls out, "Take courage! It is I. Don't be afraid." It's Jesus, defying the natural laws and walking on the very waves that threaten to capsize their boat.

Now, here's where Peter's story gets truly remarkable. In a bold, almost audacious move, Peter yells back, "Lord, if it's you, tell me to come to you on the water." Think about the guts that takes. He's not just asking for a miracle; he's asking to step into the miracle.

Jesus simply says, "Come." And Peter, with his heart pounding and adrenaline coursing through his veins, steps out of the boat. For a few incredible moments, Peter defies gravity, walking on water towards Jesus. His eyes are locked on the Savior, faith buoying each step.

But then reality crashes in. He feels the sting of the wind, sees the fury of the waves, and his human instinct kicks in. Fear floods his mind, and he begins to sink. In sheer panic, Peter cries out, "Lord, save me!"

Immediately, Jesus reaches out and grabs him. *"You of little faith,"* He says, *"why did you doubt?"* Matthew 14:31. They climb into the boat, and the wind dies down. The disciples, awestruck, worship Jesus, proclaiming, *"Truly you are the Son of God"* Matthew 14:33.

Peter's experience is a vivid reminder of our own faith journeys. He starts with an extraordinary act of faith, stepping out into the unknown, but quickly succumbs to doubt when he focuses on the storm instead of Jesus. Isn't that so relatable? We can be full of faith one moment, ready to take on the world, and paralyzed by doubt the next.

Yet, Jesus' response to Peter is what gives us hope. He doesn't let Peter drown in his fear. He immediately reaches out, rescues him, and gently questions his doubt. This tells us that Jesus is always there, ready to catch us when we falter, and gently guide us back to faith.

Peter's story isn't just about his failure; it's about the incredible faith it took to step out of the boat in the first place and the unwavering faithfulness of Jesus to catch him when he fell. It's a powerful illustration that our faith, no matter how wavering, is significant when placed in the hands of a faithful God.

Scripture to Remember

"Immediately Jesus reached out his hand and caught him. 'You of little faith,' he said, 'why did you doubt?'"
—Matthew 14:31

"But when you ask, you must believe and not doubt, because the one who doubts is like a wave of the sea, blown and tossed by the wind."
—James 1:6

"Trust in the Lord with all your heart and lean not on your own understanding."
—Proverbs 3:5

Consider This

Doubt is a natural part of the faith journey. It's through doubt that we can seek and find deeper understanding and trust in God. Like learning to ride a bike, our faith requires us to keep going, even when we fall. Trusting God means believing that He will catch us when we stumble.

Questions for Reflection

1. When have you experienced doubt in your faith journey?

_____

_____

_____

2. How did you overcome it, or how are you still working through it?

_____

_____

_____

Living Out Our Faith

Identify an area of your life where you experience doubt. Pray for God to strengthen your faith in this area and take one small step today to act in faith despite your doubt.

_____

_____

_____

_____

_____

_____

_____

Building Deeper Connection to Faith

- Journaling Prompt: Write about a time when doubt led you to seek God more earnestly. What did you learn from that experience?
- Suggested Prayer: "Lord, help me to trust in You even when doubt creeps in. Strengthen my faith and guide me through times of uncertainty. Amen."

DAY 3
FAITH IN ACTION

When I was part of a large corporate company, I joined a community project to build homes for those in need. I remember feeling out of my depth as I had no idea how to use half of the tools. But as I worked alongside others, something amazing happened. My fear and doubt were replaced by a sense of purpose and joy. Each nail I hammered and each wall we raised became a testament to the power of faith in action. It wasn't just about building houses; it was about building hope and demonstrating God's love through our efforts.

Faith isn't just a belief we hold; it's an action we take. True faith compels us to move beyond our comfort zones and into the lives of others, making a tangible difference. When we act on our faith, we become the hands and feet of Jesus, bringing His love and light to the world.

Role Models in Scripture

Consider the story of the Good Samaritan in Luke 10:25-37. Jesus tells this parable to illustrate what it means to love our neighbor. A man is traveling from Jerusalem to

Jericho when he is attacked by robbers, stripped of his clothes, beaten, and left halfdead. A priest happens to be going down the same road, but when he sees the man, he passes by on the other side. So too, a Levite, when he came to the place and saw him, passed by on the other side.

But a Samaritan, as he traveled, came where the man was, and when he saw him, he took pity on him. He went to him and bandaged his wounds, pouring on oil and wine. Then he put the man on his own donkey, brought him to an inn, and took care of him. The next day he took out two denarii and gave them to the innkeeper. 'Look after him,' he said, 'and when I return, I will reimburse you for any extra expense you may have.'

The Good Samaritan's actions are a powerful example of faith in action. Despite cultural and racial differences, the Samaritan chose compassion over convenience, mercy over indifference. He didn't just feel pity; he acted on it, even at a personal cost. This story challenges us to reflect on how we live out our faith. Do we turn away when it's inconvenient, or do we step forward to help, even when it costs us something?

Faith in action is about more than just good intentions. It's about rolling up our sleeves and getting involved, even when it's messy or challenging. It's about seeing the needs around us and responding with the love and compassion of Christ. The Good Samaritan didn't just talk about love; he demonstrated it through his actions, showing us that true faith is always accompanied by works.

Scripture to Remember

"In the same way, faith by itself, if it is not accompanied by action, is dead."
—James 2:17

"Do not merely listen to the word, and so deceive yourselves. Do what it says."
—James 1:22

"Let us not love with words or speech but with actions and in truth."
—1 John 3:18

Consider This

Faith in action means taking tangible steps to live out our beliefs. It's about more than just talking the talk; it's about walking the walk. Reflect on areas of your life where you can put your faith into action and make a difference.

Questions for Reflection

1. How can you demonstrate your faith through your actions?

_____

_____

_____

2. What barriers prevent you from living out your faith more fully?

_____

_____

_____

3. Who in your life needs to see the love of Christ through your actions today?

_____

_____

_____

4. What is one small step you can take this week to put your faith into action?

_____

_____

_____

Living Out Our Faith

Identify a specific way you can demonstrate your faith through action this week. It could be helping a neighbor, volunteering, or simply offering a kind word to someone in need. Take that step and see how God uses your actions to make an impact.

_____

_____

_____

_____

_____

_____

Building Deeper Connection to Faith

- Journaling Prompt: Reflect on a time when you put your faith into action. How did it affect you and those around you?

- Suggested Prayer: "Lord, help me to put my faith into action. Show me opportunities to serve and love others, and give me the courage to step out in faith. Amen."

Tomorrow's Journey

Today, we've explored how faith in action can transform lives. Tomorrow, we will discuss the power of faith to overcome fear. Stay committed to this journey, and let's keep building our faith together.

DAY 4
FAITH OVERCOMING FEAR

I remember the first time I had to speak in public. My hands were sweaty, my heart was racing, and I was convinced I would forget every word. The fear of standing in front of a crowd and speaking was paralyzing. But a friend reminded me of a simple truth: faith and fear cannot coexist. If I focused on my fear, it would consume me. But if I focused on my faith, I could overcome my fear. Taking a deep breath, I prayed for courage and stepped up to the podium. It wasn't perfect, but I did it, and my faith grew stronger that day.

Fear is a natural response to the unknown and the uncertain. It's something we all experience. But faith gives us the power to overcome fear, to step out in courage, and to trust God in the face of the unknown. When we choose faith over fear, we allow God to work in and through us in powerful ways.

Role Models in Scripture

One of the most inspiring stories of faith overcoming fear is the story of Joshua. After Moses' death, Joshua was appointed to lead the Israelites into the Promised Land. This was no small task. The land was filled with fortified cities and giants. The Israelites were weary and frightened. Joshua himself must have felt the weight of the responsibility. Yet, God gave Joshua a powerful command and promise: *"Be strong and courageous. Do not be afraid; do not be discouraged, for the Lord your God will be with you wherever you go."* Joshua 1:9.

Joshua took God at His word. He didn't let fear dictate his actions. Instead, he stepped forward in faith, leading the Israelites across the Jordan River and into the Promised Land. His faith was not just in his abilities, but in God's promise to be with him. Throughout the conquest of Canaan, Joshua faced numerous challenges and formidable enemies. But each time, he chose faith over fear, trusting in God's guidance and provision.

One of the most notable moments was the battle of Jericho. God's instructions were unconventional to say the least: march around the city for seven days and then blow trumpets. It must have sounded absurd to the people of Jericho and even to the Israelites. But Joshua's faith in God's plan was unwavering. They followed God's command, and the walls of Jericho came tumbling down, giving them victory.

Joshua's story teaches us that faith can lead us to victory over fear. When we trust in God's promises and follow His guidance, we can overcome the obstacles that seem insurmountable. It's not about our strength or courage, but about relying on the One who is always with us, who never leaves us nor forsakes us.

Scripture to Remember

"Be strong and courageous. Do not be afraid; do not be discouraged, for the Lord your God will be with you wherever you go."
—Joshua 1:9

"For God has not given us a spirit of fear, but of power and of love and of a sound mind."
—2 Timothy 1:7

"The Lord is my light and my salvation—whom shall I fear? The Lord is the stronghold of my life—of whom shall I be afraid?"
—Psalm 27:1

Consider This

Faith overcomes fear by focusing on God's promises and presence. Reflect on the areas of your life where fear holds you back. How can you shift your focus from fear to faith and trust in God's promises?

Questions for Reflection

1. How can you apply Joshua's example of faith to overcome your current fears?

_____

_____

_____

2. What specific promises of God can you hold onto to strengthen your faith?

_____

_____

_____

3. How has fear impacted your decisions and actions in the past?

_____

_____

_____

Living Out Our Faith

Identify a fear that is holding you back. Pray for God's strength and courage to face this fear with faith. Take a step forward, no matter how small, trusting that God is with you and will guide you through.

_____

_____

_____

_____

_____

_____

_____

Building Deeper Connection to Faith

- Journaling Prompt: Write about a time when you overcame a fear through faith. How did it change your perspective and strengthen your trust in God?
- Suggested Prayer: "Lord, help me to overcome my fears with faith. Remind me of Your promises and presence, and give me the courage to face the challenges ahead. Amen."

Tomorrow's Journey

Today, we've discussed how faith can overcome fear. Tomorrow, we will explore the relationship between faith and patience. Let's continue to grow in our faith together.

DAY 5
FAITH AND PATIENCE

Growing up, I was always impatient. Waiting for anything felt like torture, whether it was a holiday, a birthday, or even just waiting for cookies to bake. As an adult, this impatience didn't just disappear; it manifested in my spiritual life too. I wanted instant answers to my prayers, immediate results from my efforts, and quick solutions to my problems. But faith, I've learned, is often about waiting. It's about trusting God's timing and having patience even when we don't see immediate results.

Faith and patience go hand in hand. Faith trusts that God is at work, even when we can't see it. Patience waits for God's perfect timing, believing that His plans are always for our good. Together, they teach us to rely on God and to be still, knowing that He is in control.

Role Models in Scripture

Abraham's story is one of the most profound examples of faith and patience intertwined. God promised Abraham that he would be the father of many nations, that his descendants would be as numerous as the stars in the sky. Yet, Abraham and his wife Sarah were childless and advanced in age. The promise seemed impossible. Years went by, and still, there was no sign of a child. It would have been easy for Abraham to doubt, to give up, or to try to take matters into his own hands.

Indeed, at one point, Sarah suggested that Abraham have a child with her maidservant Hagar, and Ishmael was born. But this was not the child of promise. God had a specific plan and timing, and it required patience and faith. When Abraham was 100 years old, and Sarah was 90, God fulfilled His promise. Sarah gave birth to Isaac, the child of promise. It was a miraculous event that demonstrated God's faithfulness and the importance of waiting on His timing.

Abraham's faith was counted to him as righteousness because he trusted in God's promise, even when it seemed impossible. His patience was tested, but in the end, he saw the fulfillment of God's word. This story teaches us that waiting on God is never in vain. His promises are sure, and His timing is perfect.

Faith and patience together create a powerful testimony of God's faithfulness. When we trust God and wait for His timing, we demonstrate our belief in His sovereignty and His goodness. It's not always easy, but it's always worth it.

Scripture to Remember

"Yet he did not waver through unbelief regarding the promise of God, but was strengthened in his faith and gave glory to God."
—Romans 4:20

"The Lord is good to those who wait for him, to the soul who seeks him."
—Lamentations 3:25

"But if we hope for what we do not yet have, we wait for it patiently."
—Romans 8:25

Consider This

Faith and patience require trusting God's timing and His promises. Reflect on areas of your life where you struggle with impatience. How can you cultivate a deeper trust in God and wait for His perfect timing?

Questions for Reflection

1. In what areas of your life do you find it difficult to be patient?

_____

_____

_____

2. How does Abraham's story encourage you to trust God's timing?

_____

_____

_____

3. What promises of God are you holding onto as you wait?

_____

_____

_____

4. How can you develop patience in your daily walk with God?

_____

_____

_____

Living Out Our Faith

Identify an area where you need to practice patience. Spend time in prayer, asking God to help you trust His timing and to give you the patience to wait on His promises.

_____

_____

_____

_____

_____

_____

_____

Building Deeper Connection to Faith

- Journaling Prompt: Write about a time when you had to wait on God's timing. How did the experience strengthen your faith and patience?
- Suggested Prayer: "Lord, help me to trust in Your perfect timing. Give me the patience to wait on Your promises and the faith to believe that You are always at work for my good. Amen."

Tomorrow's Journey

Today, we've explored how faith and patience work together. As we wrap up this week, let's reflect on all we've learned and prepare our hearts for the journey ahead.

WEEK 1 REFLECTION

As we come to the end of Week 1, let's take a moment to
reflect together on what we've learned and how it has impacted our
journey of faith. This week has been a time of laying a solid foundation,
understanding the true nature of faith, and beginning to see how
it shapes every aspect of our lives. I hope you've felt encouraged,
challenged, and inspired just as I have. Use this space to jot down your
thoughts, insights, and any actions you plan to take moving forward.
Let's grow and learn together as we continue on this path.

Reflection Questions

1. What key insights did you gain about faith this week?

_____

_____

_____

2. How has your understanding of faith changed or deepened?

_____

_____

_____

3. In what ways have you experienced God's presence and guidance during this week?

_____

_____

_____

4. What challenges did you face, and how did you overcome them?

_____

_____

_____

5. How can you continue to build a strong foundation of faith in your daily life?

_____

_____

_____

Personal Reflections

1. What specific steps can you take to continue growing in your faith?

_____

_____

_____

2. How can you incorporate the lessons learned into your routines and habits?

_____

_____

_____

3. Are there any areas where you still struggle with maintaining faith? How can you address them?

_____

_____

_____

Action Plan

List three practical actions you will take in the coming week to nurture your faith journey.

1. _____

   _____

2. _____

   _____

3. _____

   _____

PRAYER

Spend a few moments in prayer, asking God to help you integrate what you've learned into your daily life and to continue guiding you on your journey.

"Heavenly Father, thank You for the insights and growth I've experienced this week. Help me to carry these lessons into the coming days and to live out my faith with confidence and trust in You. Strengthen my foundation of faith, and guide me as I continue this journey. Amen."

Additional Notes

Use this space to write down any additional thoughts, prayers, or reflections you have as you conclude this week.

_____

_____

_____

_____

_____

_____

_____

Preparing for Week 2

As we move into Week 2, take a moment to prepare your heart and mind for the next steps in our journey. Review the upcoming themes and consider what you hope to learn and achieve. Let's continue to build on the foundation we've established and grow deeper in our faith together.

WEEK 2
Deepening Your Faith

Welcome to Week 2 of our devotional journey. Last week, we began laying a strong foundation of faith. This week, we're going to take it a step further, exploring how we can strengthen and grow our faith in practical and meaningful ways.

I remember a time when my faith was tested in unexpected ways. I faced a series of challenges that left me feeling overwhelmed and uncertain. During this period, I realized how crucial it was to deepen my faith. I found that faith isn't just about believing in God's promises but about living them out daily, especially when life gets tough. My faith grew stronger as I leaned into God's Word, sought His presence in prayer, and surrounded myself with a community of believers who encouraged and supported me.

Deepening our faith is a continuous journey, one that we're all on together. It involves daily practices that draw us closer to God and help us rely on Him more fully. This week, we'll explore various aspects of strengthening our faith, from building a robust prayer life to engaging with Scripture in transformative ways. We'll also look at the importance of community and the role it plays in our spiritual growth.

As we embark on this week's journey, let's approach each day with an open heart and a willingness to grow. Let's dive deep together, trusting that God will meet us where we are and take us further than we ever imagined. I'm excited to walk this path with you and to see how God works in our lives as we seek to deepen our faith.

Key Themes

- The Power of Prayer: Developing a deeper, more intimate prayer life.

- Engaging with Scripture: Discovering the transformative power of God's Word.
- Living Out Faith: Practical ways to integrate faith into daily life.
- The Importance of Community: Building and nurturing a supportive faith community.
- Faith in Action: Stepping out in faith to serve and make a difference.

Anchor Scripture

"Draw near to God and He will draw near to you."
—James 4:8

Reflection

As we begin this week, reflect on your current faith practices. Are there areas where you feel your faith could be stronger? How can you deepen your relationship with God through prayer, Scripture, and community? Let's commit to this journey together, trusting that God will guide us and help us grow.

Questions for Reflection

1. What does a deeper faith look like to you?

_____

_____

_____

2. How can you enhance your prayer life this week?

_____

_____

_____

3. What steps can you take to engage more fully with Scripture?

_____

_____

_____

4. How can you build a stronger faith community around you?

_____

_____

_____

Building Deeper Connection to Faith

- Journaling Prompt: Reflect on a time when deepening your faith made a significant difference in your life. What practices helped you grow closer to God?
- Suggested Prayer: "Lord, help me to deepen my faith this week. Teach me to draw near to You in prayer, to engage with Your Word, and to build a strong community of faith around me. Strengthen my trust in You and guide me on this journey. Amen."

DAY 1
CHOSEN BY GOD

Have you ever felt overlooked or underestimated? I certainly have. Growing up in a blended family with four sisters, there were times I felt invisible or unimportant, like I was just another face in the crowd. Even now, at 60+, I sometimes struggle with feeling like I don't quite measure up. Maybe you've experienced similar moments at work, school, or even within your own family.

The idea of being chosen by God is something that I've wrestled with for a long time. That idea that not only was I seen but worthy and necessary. Is something I have to process and reprocess daily. It's not always easy to believe that the Creator of the universe sees me and has a special plan for my life. But as I've walked this journey of faith, I've come to realize that being chosen by God isn't about our worthiness or accomplishments or even our readiness. It's about His love and grace.

This week, we'll explore what it means to be chosen by God and how this truth can transform our lives. We're all on this journey together, and I'm excited to see how God uses each of us in ways we might never have imagined. Let's dive in and discover the incredible plans He has for us.

Role Models in Scripture

Esther's life began with tragedy. She was an orphan, raised by her cousin Mordecai. Growing up in exile, far from her ancestral home, Esther could have felt abandoned and insignificant. Yet, even in these humble beginnings, God had a plan for her.

Her life took an unexpected turn when King Xerxes sought a new queen. Esther, known for her beauty, was brought into the palace along with many other young women. Despite the luxury and potential for power, this was a daunting and dangerous position for Esther. Revealing her Jewish heritage could have put her at risk in a kingdom that didn't share her faith.

Esther did not initially reveal her identity as a Jew, following Mordecai's advice. She found favor with everyone, including the king, who chose her as queen. Her ascent to the throne was not just a twist of fate but a divine positioning. When Haman, a highranking official, plotted to annihilate the Jews, Mordecai urged Esther to intercede with the king.

Imagine the weight of this responsibility. Esther faced the very real possibility of death for approaching the king uninvited. It wasn't just about speaking up; it was about risking her life. Mordecai's words to her were profound: "*And who knows but that you have come to your royal position for such a time as this?*" Esther 4:14.

In a moment of profound courage, Esther called for a fast among her people, seeking God's guidance and strength. After three days, she approached the king. Here, her declaration, "If I perish, I perish," wasn't just a resignation to fate but a bold statement of faith. Esther trusted that God had placed her in this position for a purpose, even if it meant her life was at risk.

The king, moved by her bravery and the plea she presented at a series of banquets, ultimately granted her request. Haman's plot was exposed, and the Jewish people were saved. Esther's actions not only thwarted a genocide but also led to the establishment of the Jewish festival of Purim, celebrating their deliverance.

Scriptures to Remember

"You did not choose me, but I chose you and appointed you so that you might go and bear fruit—fruit that will last—and so that whatever you ask in my name the Father will give you."
—John 15:16:

"But you are a chosen people, a royal priesthood, a holy nation, God's special possession, that you may declare the praises of him who called you out of darkness into his wonderful light."
—1 Peter 2:9:

"For if you remain silent at this time, relief and deliverance for the Jews will arise from another place, but you and your father's family will perish. And who knows but that you have come to your royal position for such a time as this?"
—Esther 4:14:

Consider This

Reflect on the significance of being chosen by God. Think about Esther's courage and how her identity as God's chosen one empowered her to act. Spend time journaling about the ways you believe God has chosen and positioned you for a unique purpose.

Questions for Reflection

1. What does it mean to you to be chosen by God?

   _____

   _____

   _____

2. How has God positioned you to make a difference?

   _____

   _____

   _____

Living Out Our Faith

Identify one area in your life where you can step out in faith, trusting that God has chosen you for a purpose.

_____

_____

_____

_____

_____

_____

Building Deeper Connection to Faith

- Journaling Prompt: Reflect on how being chosen by God has influenced your life decisions. What steps can you take to embrace this identity more fully?

- Suggested Prayer: "Lord, thank You for choosing me and positioning me for a unique purpose. Help me to step out in faith and fulfill the calling You have for my life. Amen."

Tomorrow's Journey

Today, we've reflected on what it means to be chosen by God and how this impacts our actions and decisions. Tomorrow, we will delve into understanding God's love for us and how it transforms our lives. Stay open to God's leading and embrace your identity in Him.

DAY 2
FAITH AND TRUST

I'll never forget the time when I had to trust God completely during a big career shifty. Remember the DOT.com bubble? Company after company were throwing crazy money at IT certified software developers and network designers like me. I had a crazy great income job that provided very well for my family, but I felt God calling me to step out in faith and pursue a new opportunity. I could have stayed where I was and raked in the cash and bonuses and Friday pizza and beer benefits or I could listen to the prompting. I honestly could not understand why I was being called out of the "season of blessing." I mean this was a GOOOODD season, but I followed the prompt and started the journey towards a nontechbased startup. No sooner had I settled into my new job, and I was flooded with colleges asking if I knew anyone hiring. Seem that bubble I was ride burst leaving looks of people with stock options with zero and bonus never to be paid. From that experience I started to understand that trusting God meant believing that His plans for me were good, even if I couldn't see the outcome.

Trust is a crucial component of faith. It's one thing to believe in God's promises, but it's another to trust Him enough to act on them. Today, we'll explore the depth of trust in our faith journey and how trusting God can lead to incredible growth and blessings.

Role Models in Scripture

One of the most profound examples of trust in the Bible is the story of Joseph. Joseph's life was marked by a series of challenges and betrayals, yet his unwavering trust in God carried him through.

Joseph was sold into slavery by his own brothers, falsely accused by Potiphar's wife, and thrown into prison. Despite these hardships, Joseph never lost his trust in God. He believed that God had a purpose for his life, even when circumstances seemed bleak.

In Genesis 50:20, Joseph speaks to his brothers, saying, "*You intended to harm me, but God intended it for good to accomplish what is now being done, the saving of many lives.*" Joseph's trust in God's sovereignty and goodness allowed him to see beyond his suffering and recognize God's hand in his journey.

Joseph's story teaches us that trust in God means believing that He is in control, even when life doesn't make sense. It's about trusting that God's plans are good and that He can turn even the most difficult situations into something beautiful.

In our own lives, we may face situations that challenge our trust in God. We may not understand why certain things happen or how God will work them out for good. But like Joseph, we can choose to trust that God is faithful and that His plans for us are perfect.

Scripture to Remember

"Trust in the Lord with all your heart and lean not on your own understanding; in all your ways submit to him, and he will make your paths straight."
—Proverbs 3:56

"When I am afraid, I put my trust in you."
—Psalm 56:3

"And we know that in all things God works for the good of those who love him, who have been called according to his purpose."
—Romans 8:28

Consider This

Reflect on areas in your life where you struggle to trust God. How can you surrender these areas to Him and believe that He has a good plan for you? Spend time journaling about the ways you can deepen your trust in God.

Questions for Reflection

1. What does trusting God look like in your daily life?

_____

_____

_____

2. How can you deepen your trust in God's plans, especially in challenging situations?

_____

_____

_____

3. What steps can you take to surrender your fears and anxieties to God?

_____

_____

_____

Living Out Our Faith

Choose one area where you struggle to trust God. Spend time in prayer, asking Him to help you surrender this area and trust in His goodness and faithfulness.

_____

_____

_____

_____

_____

_____

Building Deeper Connection to Faith

- Journaling Prompt: Write about a time when you had to trust God in a difficult situation. How did your trust in Him impact the outcome and your faith?
- Suggested Prayer: "Lord, help me to trust You more deeply. Teach me to surrender my fears and anxieties to You, knowing that Your plans for me are good. Strengthen my faith and guide me in Your ways. Amen."

DAY 3
FAITH AND HOPE

When I was younger, I used to spend my summers with my Aunt Mable on her farm in Pennsylvania. It wasn't a fullon working farm like my other family members ran, but it was Aunt Mable's house, and she was a legend. She could split apples open with her bare hands, among other feats of wonder. One summer, Aunt Mable taught me how to plant a vegetable garden. After we had the soil perfect – Aunt Mable said that when you could smell the soil without having to pick it up, it was ready for planting. I remember feeling a mixture of excitement and fear as I placed each seed into the soil. What if the soil wasn't ready? What if I put the seed in upside down? What if I did it all wrong and nothing happened? Aunt Mable assured me that the seeds knew what to do, and with patience, care, and the right conditions, those seeds would sprout, and by the end of the summer, we would have a harvest.

Just like those seeds, faith and hope are deeply interconnected in our spiritual journey. Faith is the confidence in what we hope for, and hope is the expectation that those seeds of faith will grow and bear fruit in our lives. But along with faith and hope, there is often fear. The fear of the unknown, the fear of failure, and the fear of disappointment can all try to take root in our hearts.

Just like I feared I would plant the seeds wrong and see nothing grow, we often fear that our faith won't bear fruit. However, just as Aunt

Mable assured me, we must remember that with patience, care, and the right conditions, our faith will flourish despite our fears.

Role Models in Scripture

Just like my Aunt Mable assured me that the seeds would sprout with the right care and conditions, Abraham had to trust in God's promise despite seemingly impossible circumstances. Consider the story of Abraham, often called the father of faith. God promised Abraham that he would be the father of many nations, even though he and his wife Sarah were well beyond childbearing years. Imagine the mix of hope and fear they must have felt. Abraham's hope was rooted in God's promise, and his faith was the confidence that what God had spoken would come to pass.

In Romans 4:1821, Paul reflects on Abraham's faith and hope: *"Against all hope, Abraham in hope believed and so became the father of many nations, just as it had been said to him, 'So shall your offspring be.'* Without weakening in his faith, he faced the fact that his body was as good as dead—since he was about a hundred years old—and that Sarah's womb was also dead. Yet he did not waver through unbelief regarding the promise of God, but was strengthened in his faith and gave glory to God, being fully persuaded that God had power to do what he had promised."

Abraham's story is a testament to the power of faith and hope working together. Even when circumstances seemed impossible, Abraham held on to hope because his faith was in God's unchanging promise. His unwavering hope in God's word allowed him to remain steadfast, and ultimately, God fulfilled His promise.

This relationship between faith and hope is vital in our lives as well. When we place our hope in God and His promises, our faith is strengthened. Just as I had to trust that the seeds would grow despite my fears, we can face uncertainties and challenges with the assurance that God is faithful and will bring His promises to fruition.

Scripture to Remember

"Faith is the confidence in what we hope for and assurance about what we do not see."
—Hebrews 11:1

"May the God of hope fill you with all joy and peace as you trust in him, so that you may overflow with hope by the power of the Holy Spirit."
—Romans 15:13

"But those who hope in the Lord will renew their strength. They will soar on wings like eagles; they will run and not grow weary, they will walk and not be faint."
—Isaiah 40:31

Consider This

Reflect on the connection between faith and hope in your life. How does your hope in God's promises strengthen your faith? Spend some time journaling about the promises of God that you are holding on to and how they fuel your faith journey.

Questions for Reflection

1. How do you define the relationship between faith and hope in your spiritual life?

_____

_____

_____

2. What promises of God are you hoping for and trusting in?

_____

_____

_____

3. How can you cultivate hope in areas where you feel doubt or uncertainty?

_____

_____

_____

Living Out Our Faith

Identify one promise of God that you are hoping for. Take a small step today to act in faith, trusting that God will fulfill His promise in His timing.

_____

_____

_____

_____

_____

Building Deeper Connection to Faith

- Journaling Prompt: Write about a time when hope in God's promises strengthened your faith. How did that experience shape your relationship with God?
- Suggested Prayer: "Lord, thank You for the hope You give us through Your promises. Help me to hold on to hope and to trust that You are faithful to fulfill Your word. Strengthen my faith as I place my hope in You. Amen."

DAY 4
FAITH AND OBEDIENCE

When my son was young, I used to take him to the park to
teach him how to ride his little blue bike. At first, we would start with
the training wheels attached, and he would pedal around with so much
excitement and joy. I vividly remember the day we agreed it was time
to take off the training wheels. It was a significant step towards a "big
boy bike." Both of us felt a bit anxious. As a parent, I wanted to protect
him from falling, but I also knew that he needed to learn and grow on
his own.

That day when we arrived at the park, we worked together
taking the training wheels off his bike. It took a little bartering to get
him on the bike and promising to go really slow. As I held onto the
back of his bike, encouraging him to pedal and keep his balance. "You
can do it!" I would shout, trying to instill confidence in him. I could
see the determination in his eyes, but also the fear of falling. I assured
him that I wouldn't let him get hurt, that I was right there with him.
His trust in me led to a beautiful moment. Slowly but surely, he started
to pedal on his own, finding his balance and experiencing the joy and
freedom of riding without training wheels. The look of triumph on his
face was priceless.

This experience taught me so much about the importance
of obedience and trust in our faith journey. Just like my son had to

trust and obey my instructions to learn how to ride his bike, we need to trust and obey God's guidance in our lives. Obedience is not just about hearing God's Word but acting on it. Today, we'll explore the relationship between faith and obedience and how living out our faith through our actions can lead to spiritual growth and blessings.

Role Models in Scripture

Consider the story of Noah, a man of great faith and obedience. God instructed Noah to build an ark in preparation for a flood that would cover the earth. This command must have seemed absurd, especially since there was no immediate sign of a flood. Yet, Noah obeyed God's instructions without hesitation.

In Genesis 6:22, it is written, *"Noah did everything just as God commanded him."* Despite the ridicule and doubt from those around him, Noah's faith in God's word led him to take action. He meticulously followed God's instructions, building the ark exactly as God had specified.

Noah's obedience was a testament to his faith. He trusted that God's command was for a purpose, even if he couldn't see the full picture. His obedience not only saved his family but also preserved the future of humanity and animal life.

Imagine the scene: Noah and his family working tirelessly on this massive boat while others around them laughed and doubted. The skies were clear, and there was no sign of rain, yet Noah continued to work, driven by his unwavering faith in God's word. His neighbors probably thought he had lost his mind. Building a gigantic boat in the middle of dry land? It sounded crazy. But Noah chose to trust and obey God, believing in the unseen and the promise of God's word.

Noah's story teaches us that obedience to God requires faith, especially when His commands seem challenging or unclear. It's about trusting that God knows best and that our obedience is an expression of our faith and love for Him.

In our lives, we are often faced with choices that test our obedience to God's word. We may struggle with decisions that require us to step out of our comfort zones or go against societal norms. But like Noah, we can choose to obey God, trusting that His plans are good and that our obedience will lead to blessings.

Scripture to Remember

"Blessed rather are those who hear the word of God and obey it."
—Luke 11:28

"If you love me, keep my commands."
—John 14:15

"We know that we have come to know him if we keep his commands."
—1 John 2:3

Consider This

Reflect on areas in your life where God is calling you to obedience. How can you trust and act on His word, even when it's challenging? Spend time journaling about the ways you can live out your faith through obedience.

Questions for Reflection

1. What does obedience to God look like in your daily life?

_____

_____

_____

2. How can you deepen your obedience to God's word and commands?

_____

_____

_____

3. What steps can you take to act on God's instructions, even when they are difficult?

_____

_____

_____

Living Out Our Faith

Identify one area where God is calling you to obedience. Take a small step today to act on His word, trusting that your obedience will lead to growth and blessings.

_____

_____

_____

_____

_____

_____

Building Deeper Connection to Faith

- Journaling Prompt: Write about a time when obedience to God's word led to blessings in your life. How did this experience shape your faith and trust in Him?
- Suggested Prayer: "Lord, help me to obey Your word and commands. Teach me to trust in Your plans and to act on Your instructions, knowing that You are leading me for my good. Strengthen my faith and guide me in obedience. Amen."

DAY 5
FAITH AND ACTION

Years ago, I had the pleasure of meeting John, an older gentleman who had recently retired. John was a man brimming with stories, wisdom, and a deep faith that shone through his every word. One day, as we sat in a cozy corner of a local café, he shared a story that forever changed my view on faith in action.

John had worked hard all his life, and retirement was his time to relax and enjoy the fruits of his labor. He cherished his quiet mornings, spending hours with his wellworn Bible, a testament to his dedication. This Bible, filled with notes and highlighted passages, mirrored his journey of faith. One morning, while reading the parable of the Good Samaritan, John felt a profound nudge in his spirit.

Luke 10:3037 New International Version:

"A man was going down from Jerusalem to Jericho, when he was attacked by robbers. They stripped him of his clothes, beat him and went away, leaving him half dead. A priest happened to be going down the same road, and when he saw the man, he passed by on the other side. So too, a Levite, when he came to the place and saw him, passed by on the other side. But a Samaritan, as he traveled, came where the man was; and when he saw him, he took pity on him. He went to him and bandaged his wounds, pouring on oil and wine. Then he put the man on his own donkey, brought him to an inn and took care of him. The next day he took out two denarii

and gave them to the innkeeper. 'Look after him,' he said, 'and when I return, I will reimburse you for any extra expense you may have.'

"Which of these three do you think was a neighbor to the man who fell into the hands of robbers?"

The expert in the law replied, "The one who had mercy on him."

Jesus told him, "Go and do likewise."

As John reflected on this parable, he realized that while he enjoyed his comfortable life, he wasn't truly living out his faith. The message about loving your neighbor and taking action resonated deeply. He understood that faith required more than just reading and praying; it demanded action.

A few days later, John noticed a flyer about a local food pantry needing volunteers. His initial reaction was to ignore it, citing his busy schedule and commitments. But the nudge in his heart persisted, reminding him of the Good Samaritan's compassion and action. He decided to step out in faith and volunteer.

John's first day at the food pantry was eyeopening. He met people from all walks of life, each with their own struggles and stories. Packing food boxes and offering a listening ear seemed small, but he quickly realized the impact these simple acts had. He began to form connections with the people he served, offering not just food, but encouragement and prayer.

One cold winter day, a young mother came in with her two children. They were clearly struggling, and John's heart went out to them. He helped them get warm clothing and connected them with resources for housing. Over time, he witnessed the family's transformation and their journey towards selfsufficiency.

This experience profoundly changed John. He realized that faith in action was about embodying God's love in tangible ways. It wasn't just about good deeds; it was about living out his faith through compassionate action. John's story is a powerful reminder that when we step out in faith and act on God's nudges, we not only bless others but also grow and deepen our own faith.

Faith in action means living out our beliefs daily. Today, let's explore how our actions can reflect our faith and impact our spiritual growth and the world around us.

Role Models in Scripture

By enhancing the narrative structure and emotional depth, the story becomes more engaging and instructional, illustrating the theme of faith in action more vividly. James, the brother of Jesus, is a powerful advocate for faith in action. In his epistle, he emphasizes that faith without deeds is dead. James 2:1417 says, *"What good is it, my brothers and sisters, if someone claims to have faith but has no deeds? Can such faith save them? Suppose a brother or a sister is without clothes and daily food. If one of you says to them, 'Go in peace; keep warm and well fed,' but does nothing about their physical needs, what good is it? In the same way, faith by itself, if it is not accompanied by action, is dead."*

James' words are a call to active faith. He challenges believers to demonstrate their faith through their actions. This doesn't mean that deeds earn salvation but that genuine faith naturally produces good works. Our actions reflect the authenticity of our faith and our commitment to living out God's commands.

Consider the story of the Good Samaritan in Luke 10:2537. A man was beaten and left halfdead on the side of the road. Two religious leaders passed by without helping, but a Samaritan, moved by compassion, stopped to care for the man. He bandaged his wounds, took him to an inn, and paid for his care. Jesus used this parable to illustrate that love and compassion should be at the heart of our actions.

The Samaritan's actions were a powerful expression of faith in action. He didn't just feel compassion; he acted on it, providing tangible help to someone in need. His example teaches us that living out our faith means stepping out of our comfort zones and serving others with love and compassion.

In our daily lives, we encounter countless opportunities to put our faith into action. It could be through acts of kindness, volunteering, supporting those in need, or simply being present for someone who is struggling. When we act on our faith, we become vessels of God's love and grace, impacting the world around us.

Scripture to Remember

"In the same way, faith by itself, if it is not accompanied by action, is dead."
—James 2:17

"Let us not love with words or speech but with actions and in truth."
—1 John 3:18

"You see that his faith and his actions were working together, and his faith was made complete by what he did."
—James 2:22

Consider This

Reflect on how you can put your faith into action. What are some practical ways you can serve others and live out your faith daily?

Spend time journaling about the opportunities God has placed before you to demonstrate His love through your actions.

Questions for Reflection

1. What does faith in action look like in your life?

_____

_____

_____

2. How can you demonstrate your faith through your actions this week?

_____

_____

_____

3. What steps can you take to serve others and show God's love in practical ways?

_____

_____

_____

Living Out Our Faith

Identify one specific action you can take today to live out your faith. It could be helping someone in need, volunteering, or showing kindness to a stranger. Take that step and trust that God will work through your actions.

_____

_____

_____

_____

_____

_____

Building Deeper Connection to Faith

- Journaling Prompt: Write about a time when acting on your faith made a difference in your life or someone else's. How did it impact your relationship with God and others?
- Suggested Prayer: "Lord, help me to live out my faith through my actions. Teach me to serve others with love and compassion, and let my deeds reflect Your grace and truth. Strengthen my faith and guide me as I put it into practice. Amen."

WEEK 2 REFLECTION

As we come to the end of Week 2, take some time to reflect on what you have learned and how it has impacted your journey of faith. This week, we delved deeper into strengthening our faith, understanding the importance of trust, hope, and obedience. Use this space to jot down your thoughts, insights, and any actions you plan to take moving forward. Let's reflect together and continue to grow in our faith.

Reflection Questions

1. What key insights did you gain about faith, trust, and obedience this week?

_____

_____

_____

2. How has your understanding of faith deepened?

_____

_____

_____

3. In what ways have you experienced God's presence and guidance during this week?

_____

_____

_____

4. What challenges did you face, and how did you overcome them?

_____

_____

_____

5. How can you continue to build a strong foundation of faith in your daily life?

_____

_____

_____

Personal Reflections

1. What specific steps can you take to continue growing in your faith?

_____

_____

_____

2. How can you incorporate the lessons learned into your routines and habits?

_____

_____

_____

3. Are there any areas where you still struggle with maintaining faith? How can you address them?

_____

_____

_____

Action Plan

List three practical actions you will take in the coming week to nurture your faith journey.

1. _____

_____

2. _____

_____

3. _____

_____

PRAYER

Spend a few moments in prayer, asking God to help you integrate what you've learned into your daily life and to continue guiding you on your journey.

"Heavenly Father, thank You for the insights and growth I've experienced this week. Help me to carry these lessons into the coming days and to live out my faith with confidence and trust in You. Strengthen my foundation of faith and guide me as I continue this journey. Amen."

Additional Notes

Use this space to write down any additional thoughts, prayers, or reflections you have as you conclude this week.

_____

_____

_____

_____

_____

_____

Preparing for Week 3

As we move into Week 3, take a moment to prepare your heart and mind for the next steps in our journey. Review the upcoming themes and consider what you hope to learn and achieve. Let's continue to build on the foundation we've established and grow deeper in our faith together.

WEEK 3
Living Out Faith in
Daily Life

Welcome to Week 3 of our devotional journey. We've spent the last two weeks building a solid foundation of faith and exploring ways to deepen that faith. This week, we'll focus on living out our faith in practical, everyday ways. It's about taking what we believe and making it visible in our actions, decisions, and interactions with others.

I remember a time when I felt God nudging me to step out and put my faith into action. It wasn't a grand mission or a huge life change, but a simple, everyday moment that challenged me to live out my beliefs. I was at the grocery store, of all places, and I noticed an elderly woman struggling with her bags. Normally, I might have smiled politely and gone on my way, but this time I felt a strong urge to help. I offered her assistance, carried her bags to her car, and spent a few minutes chatting with her. She shared stories about her late husband and her love for her grandchildren. That small act of kindness turned into a meaningful connection that brightened both our days.

This week, we'll explore how living out our faith doesn't always mean doing big, extraordinary things. Often, it's about the small, everyday actions that reflect God's love and grace to those around us. We'll look at ways to integrate faith into our daily routines, make a positive impact in our communities, and become a living testimony of God's goodness.

Key Themes

- Everyday Faith: Finding opportunities to live out faith in daily routines and interactions.
- Faith and Service: Serving others as an expression of faith.
- Faith in Relationships: Reflecting God's love in our relationships with family, friends, and colleagues.

- Faith and Integrity: Upholding integrity and honesty in all aspects of life.
- Faith and Joy: Embracing joy and gratitude as part of a faith filled life.

Anchor Scripture

"Let your light shine before others, that they may see your good deeds and glorify your Father in heaven."
—Matthew 5:16

Reflection

As we embark on this week's journey, reflect on the ways you can let your faith shine in your daily life. How can you make your beliefs visible through your actions and interactions? Let's commit to living out our faith in practical ways that honor God and bless those around us.

Questions for Reflection

1. What does living out your faith look like in your daily life?

_____

_____

_____

2. How can you serve others as an expression of your faith?

_____

_____

_____

3. In what ways can you reflect God's love in your relationships?

_____

_____

_____

4. How can you uphold integrity and honesty in all aspects of your life?

_____

_____

_____

Building Deeper Connection to Faith

Journaling Prompt: Reflect on a recent experience where you lived out your faith in a small but meaningful way. What did you learn from that experience?

_____

_____

_____

_____

_____

Suggested Prayer

"Lord, help me to live out my faith in my daily life. Teach me to serve others, reflect Your love, uphold integrity, and embrace joy and gratitude. Guide my actions so that they may honor You and bless those around me. Amen."

DAY 1
EVERYDAY FAITH

When I was about twelve, I spent a lot of time helping my grandpa in his small workshop. He wasn't a master carpenter or anything, but he loved making wooden boxes and furniture. His workshop was a place of wonder for me, filled with the smell of sawdust and the hum of tools. What stood out to me the most wasn't just the projects we worked on but the way my grandpa approached each task.

Every time we finished a piece, no matter how simple or small, he would take a moment to pray over it. He'd say, "God, bless whoever receives this. May it bring joy and serve its purpose well." It was such a small gesture, but it left a huge impression on me. My grandpa taught me that faith isn't just about the big, grand moments but about the small, intentional actions we take every day.

I remember one particular project vividly. We were making a set of wooden blocks for a local daycare. It was a simple task, but grandpa approached it with the same care and reverence as if we were crafting a masterpiece. As we sanded the edges and painted the blocks in bright, cheerful colors, he shared stories from his life, weaving in lessons about faith, love, and service. He would often say, "Eric, it's not the size of the task that matters, but the heart behind it."

One day, while we were working, a neighbor stopped by to borrow a tool. Instead of just handing it over, grandpa invited him in, and took the time to listen to his concerns. It was a small act of kindness, but it spoke volumes about living out faith in everyday interactions. Watching him, I realized that faith wasn't something to be confined to church or big events; it was woven into the fabric of daily life.

Faith isn't just for Sundays or special occasions. It's something we live out every day, in everything we do. Whether it's showing kindness to a stranger, being patient with a coworker, or taking time to pray and reflect, our faith should be evident in all aspects of our lives. Today, we'll explore how to integrate faith into our daily routines and make it a natural part of who we are.

Role Models in Scripture

Consider the story of Ruth, a woman whose everyday faithfulness and loyalty had a profound impact. After the death of her husband, Ruth chose to stay with her mother-in-law, Naomi, instead of returning to her own family. This decision wasn't driven by a grand vision or a divine encounter, but by her deep commitment and faithfulness.

Ruth 1:16-17 captures her devotion: *"But Ruth replied, 'Don't urge me to leave you or to turn back from you. Where you go I will go, and where you stay I will stay. Your people will be my people and your God my God. Where you die I will die, and there I will be buried. May the Lord deal with me, be it ever so severely, if even death separates you and me.'"*

Ruth's faith was demonstrated through her actions, her loyalty, and her willingness to step into the unknown. She didn't seek recognition or reward; she simply lived out her faith in her everyday decisions. Her story shows us that everyday faithfulness can lead to extraordinary outcomes. Ruth's loyalty and hard work eventually caught the attention of Boaz, a man of great character, leading to her becoming the great-grandmother of King David and part of the lineage of Jesus.

In our own lives, we might not see the immediate impact of our everyday faithfulness, but God does. Each small act of kindness, each moment of patience, and each decision to do what's right reflects our faith and can have a lasting impact beyond what we can see.

Scripture to Remember

"And whatever you do, whether in word or deed, do it all in the name of the Lord Jesus, giving thanks to God the Father through him."
—Colossians 3:17

"So whether you eat or drink or whatever you do, do it all for the glory of God."
—1 Corinthians 10:31

"Let your light shine before others, that they may see your good deeds and glorify your Father in heaven."
—Matthew 5:16

Consider This

Reflect on how you can live out your faith in your daily routines. What small actions can you take to show God's love and care to those around you? Spend time journaling about the everyday opportunities you have to let your faith shine.

Questions for Reflection

1. How can you integrate your faith into your daily routines?

_____

_____

_____

2. What small actions can you take to reflect God's love and care?

_____

_____

_____

3. How can you be more intentional about living out your faith every day?

_____

_____

_____

Living Out Our Faith

Identify one small action you can take today to live out your faith. It could be helping a neighbor, showing kindness to a stranger, or spending extra time in prayer. Commit to doing it and see how it impacts your day.

_____

_____

_____

_____

_____

Building Deeper Connection to Faith

- Journaling Prompt: Write about a time when you saw the impact of living out your faith in a small but meaningful way. How did it make you feel, and what did you learn from it?
- Suggested Prayer: "Lord, help me to live out my faith in my daily life. Teach me to see the opportunities to reflect Your love and care in small actions. Guide me to be faithful in the everyday moments, knowing that You see and value each one. Amen."

DAY 2
FAITH AND SERVICE

When I was younger, I often heard stories about a man named Mr. Thompson, a fictional character who always found himself in heartwarming and thought-provoking situations. Mr. Thompson was known for his extraordinary ability to find joy and purpose in the small, everyday moments of life, especially through acts of service.

One story that particularly resonated with me was about Mr. Thompson's involvement in his community. Every Saturday morning, without fail, he would head to the local park to pick up litter and chat with the people he met along the way. It wasn't a grand gesture, but it was his way of giving back and making his neighborhood a better place.

One chilly autumn morning, Mr. Thompson noticed a young girl sitting alone on a park bench, tears streaming down her face. Concerned, he approached her and gently asked if she was okay. The girl, hesitant at first, eventually opened up about how she felt invisible and unimportant at school. Mr. Thompson listened patiently, offering words of encouragement and sharing stories of his own childhood struggles.

Before leaving, he handed the girl a small notebook. "This helped me when I was your age," he said. "Write down your thoughts and dreams. Sometimes, putting them on paper can help you see things more clearly." The girl's face lit up with gratitude, and from that day on, she and Mr. Thompson formed a unique bond, meeting every Saturday to talk and write together.

This story about Mr. Thompson highlights how service is a powerful expression of faith. It's not just about grand gestures; it's about the small, consistent actions that reflect God's love and care. Mr. Thompson didn't set out to change the world, but through his simple acts of kindness, he made a significant impact on those around him.

Faith and service are deeply interconnected. Our faith should naturally lead us to serve others, and in doing so, we live out God's love in tangible ways. Today, we'll explore how service plays a crucial role in our faith journey and how it can bring us closer to God and to each other.

Role Models in Scripture

Consider the story of the Good Samaritan in Luke 10:25-37. This parable starts with a man traveling from Jerusalem to Jericho who unfortunately crosses paths with robbers. They strip him of his clothes, beat him up, and leave him half-dead on the side of the road. Imagine lying there, vulnerable, and in desperate need of help. Then, along comes hope in the form of a priest and a Levite. Surely, these religious leaders will stop to help, right? Nope. Both of them, seeing the man, decide to cross to the other side of the road and continue on their way, leaving the man to his fate. Their actions or inactions highlight a stark contrast between religious duty and true compassion.

And then, drumroll please, a Samaritan comes along. Now, to fully grasp the significance, you need to understand that Samaritans were the sworn enemies of the Jews at the time. They were considered outsiders and were often despised. Despite this deep-seated animosity, the Samaritan is moved by compassion when he sees the wounded man.

He doesn't just think, "Poor guy, hope someone helps him." He acts! The Samaritan bandages the man's wounds, using oil and wine to clean and soothe them. He then puts the man on his own donkey, essentially giving up his ride to help the stranger. He takes him to an inn and takes care of him. And get this: the Samaritan even pays the innkeeper to continue looking after the man, promising to cover any extra costs on his return trip. Talk about going the extra mile!

Jesus used this parable to hammer home a crucial point: love and compassion should be at the heart of our actions. The Samaritan's response is a masterclass in faith in action. He didn't just feel bad for the guy; he took tangible steps to help. His example shows us that living out our faith means stepping out of our comfort zones and serving others with love and compassion, no matter the social or cultural barriers.

In our daily lives, we bump into endless chances to put our faith into action. It could be simple acts like helping a neighbor carry their groceries, volunteering at a local shelter, or even just lending an ear to a friend who's having a rough day. These acts, though they might seem small, can have a monumental impact. They reflect God's love and grace, transforming not only the lives of those we help but also our own hearts.

The Good Samaritan's story dares us to look in the mirror and ask ourselves some tough questions. Are we willing to stop and help, even when it's inconvenient or uncomfortable? Do we see those in need as our neighbors, deserving of our love and care? When we act on our faith, we become vessels of God's love, impacting the world around us in ways we may never fully grasp.

This parable also serves as a reminder that true faith isn't just about rituals or religious titles; it's about how we treat others, especially those different from us or whom society tends to overlook. By following the Samaritan's example, we live out Jesus' command to "love your neighbor as yourself," showing that our faith is vibrant and active, deeply rooted in love and compassion.

Scripture to Remember

"Each of you should use whatever gift you have received to serve others, as faithful stewards of God's grace in its various forms."
—1 Peter 4:10

"The greatest among you will be your servant."
—Matthew 23:11

"For even the Son of Man did not come to be served, but to serve, and to give his life as a ransom for many."
—Mark 10:45

Consider This

Reflect on the ways you can serve others in your daily life. How can you use your gifts and talents to meet the needs of those around you? Spend time journaling about the opportunities God has placed before you to serve and make a difference.

Questions for Reflection

1. What does service look like in your daily life?

_____

_____

_____

2. How can you use your gifts and talents to serve others?

_____

_____

_____

3. What steps can you take to make service a regular part of your faith journey?

_____

_____

_____

Living Out Our Faith

Identify one specific act of service you can perform this week. It could be volunteering, helping a neighbor, or offering support to a friend in need. Commit to doing it and see how it strengthens your faith and impacts those around you.

_____

_____

_____

_____

_____

_____

Building Deeper Connection to Faith

- Journaling Prompt: Write about a time when you served others and felt God's presence in a special way. How did it impact your faith and your relationship with God?

- Suggested Prayer: "Lord, help me to serve others with love and compassion. Teach me to use my gifts and talents to meet the needs of those around me. Strengthen my faith as I step out in service and show Your love in practical ways. Amen."

DAY 3
FAITH IN RELATIONSHIPS

I remember when I first got married, I thought I had it all figured out. My partner and I were madly in love, and I was convinced that our relationship would be smooth sailing. We were like two peas in a pod, and nothing could go wrong. But as any married couple can tell you, it didn't take long for reality to set in. We faced challenges and disagreements, and I quickly realized that maintaining a healthy, loving relationship required more than just good intentions. It required faith, patience, and a lot of grace.

Let me tell you about one particular rough patch we hit. We were both juggling busy careers and felt the strain of trying to keep our connection strong amidst the chaos. One evening, after a particularly heated argument about something trivial I think it was about whose turn it was to take out the trash, I took a long walk to clear my head. During that walk, I had a moment of clarity. I realized that our relationship was not just about the two of us; it was also about our faith and how we reflected God's love, grace, and forgiveness to each other.

That evening, I decided to approach our relationship differently. Instead of focusing on winning arguments or proving points, I focused on understanding and patience. I prayed for guidance and asked God to help me love my partner better, to show grace in moments of frustration, and to be a reflection of His love.

Relationships are a crucial part of our faith journey. They provide opportunities to reflect God's love, grace, and forgiveness. Today, we'll explore how our faith can strengthen our relationships and help us navigate the ups and downs of life with love and compassion.

Faith in relationships isn't just about grand gestures. It's about small, everyday actions that build trust and intimacy. It's about choosing to listen when you'd rather speak, offering a hug when you'd rather walk away, and finding moments to pray together even when you're exhausted. It's about recognizing that both of you are imperfect and will make mistakes, but through faith and love, you can grow stronger together.

Faith also teaches us the importance of forgiveness in relationships. Holding onto grudges or past hurts only creates a barrier between us and those we love. Forgiving my partner, and seeking forgiveness when I was in the wrong, became essential steps in our journey together. It wasn't always easy, but each act of forgiveness brought us closer and reminded us of the grace we receive from God every day.

Today, I encourage you to reflect on your relationships. How can your faith help you navigate the ups and downs with love and compassion? How can you show God's love, grace, and forgiveness in your interactions with others? Spend some time thinking about these questions and see how your faith can bring new strength and depth to your relationships.

Role Models in Scripture

Consider the relationship between Jonathan and David, one of the most remarkable friendships in the Bible. Despite the fact that Jonathan's father, King Saul, saw David as a threat and sought to kill him, Jonathan and David formed a deep bond based on mutual respect, loyalty, and faith in God.

1 Samuel 18:1-4 describes their friendship: *"After David had finished talking with Saul, Jonathan became one in spirit with David, and he loved him as himself. From that day Saul kept David with him and did not let him return home to his family. And Jonathan made a covenant with David because he loved him as himself. Jonathan took off the robe he was wearing and gave it to David, along with his tunic, and even his sword, his bow and his belt."*

Their friendship was tested many times, especially as Saul's jealousy and anger towards David grew. Despite the danger, Jonathan remained loyal to David, warning him of his father's plans and helping him escape. Jonathan's faithfulness and love for David were grounded in his trust in God's plan and his understanding of true friendship.

This story teaches us about the importance of faith in our relationships. It shows us that genuine relationships are built on trust, loyalty, and selflessness. Jonathan's willingness to risk his own safety for David's wellbeing reflects the kind of love and faithfulness that God calls us to have in our relationships.

Scripture to Remember

"A friend loves at all times, and a brother is born for a time of adversity."
—Proverbs 17:17

"Above all, love each other deeply, because love covers over a multitude of sins."
—1 Peter 4:8

"Be completely humble and gentle; be patient, bearing with one another in love."
—Ephesians 4:2

Consider This

Reflect on your relationships and how your faith influences them. How can you show God's love, grace, and forgiveness in your interactions with others? Spend time journaling about the ways you can strengthen your relationships through your faith.

Questions for Reflection

1. How does your faith influence your relationships?

_____

_____

_____

2. What steps can you take to show God's love and grace in your interactions with others?

_____

_____

_____

3. How can you strengthen your relationships through faith and prayer?

_____

_____

_____

Living Out Our Faith

Identify one relationship in your life that could benefit from a little extra faith and love. Take a specific action this week to show kindness, support, or forgiveness in that relationship.

_____

_____

_____

_____

_____

_____

Building Deeper Connection to Faith

- Journaling Prompt: Write about a time when your faith helped you navigate a challenging relationship. How did it impact your relationship and your faith?
- Suggested Prayer: "Lord, help me to reflect Your love and grace in my relationships. Teach me to be patient, kind, and forgiving, and to strengthen my connections through faith and prayer. Guide me as I seek to build healthy, loving relationships that honor You. Amen."

DAY 4
FAITH AND CHALLENGES

I'll never forget the first time I volunteered at a local food pantry. I was nervous and unsure of what to expect. What if I didn't know what to do? What if I messed up? But as soon as I walked through the doors, I was greeted with warmth and gratitude. The experience of serving others, of being part of something bigger than myself, was transformative. I realized that serving wasn't just about giving my time; it was about living out my faith in a tangible way.

Faith isn't just for the good times; it's for the challenges and hardships too. It's easy to have faith when everything is going well, but the true test of faith comes when we face difficulties. Today, we'll explore how our faith can sustain us through life's challenges and how we can grow stronger in our faith during tough times.

Role Models in Scripture

Consider the story of Job, a man who faced immense suffering yet remained faithful to God. Job was a wealthy man with a large family, but he lost everything—his children, his wealth, and his health. Despite his suffering, Job did not turn away from God. Instead, he continued to trust in God's goodness and sovereignty.

Job 1:20-22 describes Job's reaction to his losses: *"At this, Job got up and tore his robe and shaved his head. Then he fell to the ground in worship and said: 'Naked I came from my mother's womb, and naked I will depart. The Lord gave and the Lord has taken away; may the name of the Lord be praised.' In all this, Job did not sin by charging God with wrongdoing."*

Job's faith in the midst of suffering teaches us that we can trust God even when we don't understand our circumstances. His story shows us that faith is not dependent on our situation but on our relationship with God. Job's unwavering trust in God, despite his immense suffering, is a powerful example of faith in action.

In our own lives, we will face challenges and hardships. Our faith will be tested, and we may not always understand why things happen. But like Job, we can choose to trust God and remain faithful. We can believe that God is with us, even in the darkest times, and that He has a purpose for our suffering.

Scripture to Remember

"Consider it pure joy, my brothers and sisters, whenever you face trials of many kinds, because you know that the testing of your faith produces perseverance."
—James 1:2-3

"And we know that in all things God works for the good of those who love him, who have been called according to his purpose."
—Romans 8:28

"The Lord is close to the brokenhearted and saves those who are crushed in spirit."
—Psalm 34:18

Consider This

Reflect on the challenges you have faced and how your faith has sustained you. How can you trust God more deeply during difficult times? Spend time journaling about the ways God has worked in your life through challenges and how you can grow stronger in your faith.

Questions for Reflection

1. How has your faith sustained you through challenges?

_____

_____

_____

2. What steps can you take to trust God more deeply during difficult times?

_____

_____

_____

3. How can you grow stronger in your faith through life's challenges?

_____

_____

_____

Living Out Our Faith

Identify one challenge you are currently facing and commit to trusting God with it. Spend time in prayer, asking God to strengthen your faith and help you see His purpose in your suffering.

_____

_____

_____

_____

_____

Building Deeper Connection to Faith

- Journaling Prompt: Write about a time when you faced a significant challenge and how your faith helped you through it. What did you learn from that experience?
- Suggested Prayer: "Lord, help me to trust You more deeply during difficult times. Strengthen my faith and remind me of Your presence and purpose in my suffering. Guide me and give me the courage to remain faithful, knowing that You are with me always. Amen."

DAY 5
FAITH AND ACTION

Years ago, I became a foster parent, opening my home and heart to children in need. It was a challenging yet incredibly rewarding journey. Balancing work, family, and the demands of fostering was no easy task, but I felt a deep calling to provide a safe and loving environment for these children. My days were full, my schedule was tight, and yet, I felt another nudge from God pushing me towards a greater commitment.

One evening, after a particularly busy day, I received a call asking if I would consider stepping into the role of president for our county's foster and parent association. My initial reaction was to decline—I had every excuse ready. My schedule was already overflowing, I had other commitments, and I didn't feel equipped to take on such a significant responsibility. But the more I thought about it, the stronger the nudge became. I realized that leading by example and advocating for foster children and parents was a profound way to live out my faith.

Despite my hesitations, I decided to step out in faith and accept the role. My first few weeks as president were overwhelming. There were meetings to attend, initiatives to organize, and countless families to support. But with each passing day, I saw the impact of our collective efforts. We launched programs to provide additional resources for foster families, organized support groups, and worked on policies to improve the foster care system in our county.

One particular event stands out in my memory. We organized a community fair to raise awareness about fostering and to recruit more families. My son and the other foster children were deeply involved, helping with the setup and engaging with the community. Seeing their enthusiasm and hearing their stories of how fostering had impacted their lives was incredibly moving. It was a powerful reminder of why this work was so important.

Through my role as president, I met many dedicated and compassionate people. One such person was Linda, a foster mother who had taken in over twenty children throughout her life. Her unwavering faith and commitment were truly inspiring. She shared how her faith guided her every step and how she believed that every child deserved love and a chance to thrive. Her story reinforced the importance of our mission and the power of faith in action.

This experience profoundly changed me. I realized that faith in action was about embodying God's love in tangible ways, even when it seemed impossible. It wasn't just about good deeds; it was about living out my faith through compassionate leadership and advocacy. By stepping into this role, I not only blessed others but also grew and deepened my own faith.

Through this journey, I learned that faith in action means living out our beliefs daily. It's not enough to simply believe; we must also act on our faith. By leading the foster and parent association, I saw firsthand how our actions can reflect our faith and impact our spiritual growth and the world around us. Today, let's explore how we can put our faith into practice and make a difference in our communities.

Role Models in Scripture

James, the brother of Jesus, is a powerful advocate for faith in action. In his epistle, he emphasizes that faith without deeds is dead. James 2:14-17 says, *"What good is it, my brothers and sisters, if someone claims to have faith but has no deeds? Can such faith save them? Suppose a brother or a sister is without clothes and daily food. If one of you says to them, 'Go in peace; keep warm and well fed,' but does nothing about their physical needs, what good is it? In the same way, faith by itself, if it is not accompanied by action, is dead."*

James' words are a call to active faith. He challenges believers to demonstrate their faith through their actions. This doesn't mean that deeds earn salvation but that genuine faith naturally produces good works. Our actions reflect the authenticity of our faith and our commitment to living out God's commands.

Consider the story of the Good Samaritan in Luke 10:25-37. A man was beaten and left half-dead on the side of the road. Two religious leaders passed by without helping, but a Samaritan, moved by compassion, stopped to care for the man. He bandaged his wounds, took him to an inn, and paid for his care. Jesus used this parable to illustrate that love and compassion should be at the heart of our actions.

The Samaritan's actions were a powerful expression of faith in action. He didn't just feel compassion; he acted on it, providing tangible help to someone in need. His example teaches us that living out our faith means stepping out of our comfort zones and serving others with love and compassion.

In our daily lives, we encounter countless opportunities to put our faith into action. It could be through acts of kindness, volunteering, supporting those in need, or simply being present for someone who is struggling. When we act on our faith, we become vessels of God's love and grace, impacting the world around us.

Scripture to Remember

"In the same way, faith by itself, if it is not accompanied by action, is dead."
—James 2:17

"Let us not love with words or speech but with actions and in truth."
—1 John 3:18

"You see that his faith and his actions were working together, and his faith was made complete by what he did."
—James 2:22

Consider This

Reflect on how you can put your faith into action. What are some practical ways you can serve others and live out your faith daily? Spend time journaling about the opportunities God has placed before you to demonstrate His love through your actions.

Questions for Reflection

1. What does faith in action look like in your life?

_____

_____

_____

2. How can you demonstrate your faith through your actions this week?

_____

_____

_____

3. What steps can you take to serve others and show God's love in practical ways?

_____

_____

_____

Living Out Our Faith

Identify one specific action you can take today to live out your faith. It could be helping someone in need, volunteering, or showing kindness to a stranger. Take that step and trust that God will work through your actions.

Building Deeper Connection to Faith

- Journaling Prompt: Write about a time when acting on your faith made a difference in your life or someone else's. How did it impact your relationship with God and others?
- Suggested Prayer: "Lord, help me to live out my faith through my actions. Teach me to serve others with love and compassion, and let my deeds reflect Your grace and truth. Strengthen my faith and guide me as I put it into practice. Amen."

WEEK 3 REFLECTION

As we come to the end of Week 3, take some time to reflect on what you have learned and how it has impacted your journey of faith. This week, we delved deeper into living out our faith, understanding the importance of everyday faith, service, and action. Use this space to jot down your thoughts, insights, and any actions you plan to take moving forward. Let's reflect together and continue to grow in our faith.

Reflection Questions

1. What key insights did you gain about living out your faith this week?

_____

_____

_____

2. How has your understanding of faith in action deepened?

_____

_____

_____

3. In what ways have you experienced God's presence and guidance during this week?

_____

_____

_____

4. What challenges did you face, and how did you overcome them?

_____

_____

_____

5. How can you continue to build a strong foundation of faith in your daily life?

_____

_____

_____

Personal Reflections

1. What specific steps can you take to continue growing in your faith?

_____

_____

_____

2. How can you incorporate the lessons learned into your routines and habits?

_____

_____

_____

3. Are there any areas where you still struggle with maintaining faith? How can you address them?

_____

_____

_____

Action Plan

List three practical actions you will take in the coming week to nurture your faith journey.

1. _____

_____

2. _____

_____

3. _____

_____

PRAYER

Spend a few moments in prayer, asking God to help you integrate what you've learned into your daily life and to continue guiding you on your journey.

"Heavenly Father, thank You for the insights and growth I've experienced this week. Help me to carry these lessons into the coming days and to live out my faith with confidence and trust in You. Strengthen my foundation of faith and guide me as I continue this journey. Amen."

Additional Notes

Use this space to write down any additional thoughts, prayers, or reflections you have as you conclude this week.

_____

_____

_____

_____

_____

_____

PRAYER FOR FAITH
Strengthening Your Relationship with God

Opening:
> "Heavenly Father, I come before You with a humble heart, recognizing Your greatness and the depth of Your love for me."

Thanksgiving:
> "Thank You, Lord, for guiding me through this journey of strengthening my faith. I am grateful for the wisdom and insights You have provided along the way."

Reflection:
> "Lord, I have learned that true faith is built on trust in Your promises, understanding Your Word, and cultivating a relationship with You through prayer and spiritual disciplines. I recognize the importance of daily commitment to growing my faith."

Petitions:

"Father, I ask for Your strength and guidance as I continue to deepen my faith. Help me to trust in Your promises and rely on Your strength, especially in times of doubt and difficulty. Fill me with Your Spirit so that I may walk by faith and not by sight."

Commitment:

"I commit to nurturing my faith each day, dedicating time to prayer, scripture reading, and reflection. Help me to stay rooted in Your Word and to live out my faith in every aspect of my life."

Intercession:

"I also lift up those who are struggling in their faith. May they find comfort and assurance in You. Use me, Lord, to support and encourage them in their spiritual journey."

Closing:

"I ask all these things in the precious name of Jesus Christ, my Savior. Amen."

ADDITIONAL RESOURCES

Books and Articles
    Books: Suggested readings for deeper understanding.

    The Purpose Driven Life by Rick Warren
    This bestselling book offers a 40day spiritual journey that will help you discover and live out God's purpose for your life. It provides practical insights and biblical principles to guide you in understanding your identity and calling.

    Faith: Living a Life of Faith by T.D. Jakes
    In this empowering book, T.D. Jakes explores the concept of faith from a biblical perspective, encouraging readers to embrace their faith in God and live out their unique purpose with confidence and conviction.

    Crazy Love: Overwhelmed by a Relentless God by Francis Chan
    This book delves into the biblical truths about God's love and how it transforms our faith, providing a clear and concise exploration of our relationship with God as believers. It's a great resource for anyone looking to deepen their understanding of their faith.

Grace for the Moment by Max Lucado

This daily devotional offers inspiring and uplifting messages that remind us of God's grace and how it sustains our faith. It's perfect for daily reflections and encouragement.

Articles: Recommended articles for further insight.

"Strengthening Your Faith in God" on Desiring God

This insightful article from Desiring God delves into the importance of strengthening our faith in God rather than relying on worldly solutions. It offers practical advice and biblical wisdom on how to root our sense of faith in God's truth.

"Understanding Faith and Trust in God" on Crosswalk

Crosswalk provides a comprehensive article that explores the concept of faith and trust in God, highlighting key scriptures and practical steps to help believers embrace and live out their true faith in God.

"Growing Your Faith: Practical Steps" on Bible Study Tools

This article discusses practical ways to grow your faith daily, providing actionable advice and scriptural support to help you walk confidently in your faith.

"You Are More Than What You Do: Finding Your Faith in God" on Relevant Magazine

Relevant Magazine offers an engaging article that addresses the struggle of defining ourselves by our achievements and encourages readers to find their true faith in God.

Online Resources Websites:

Desiring God www.desiringgod.org

Desiring God offers a wealth of articles, sermons, and resources focused on helping believers find joy and purpose in God. It's a great site for deepening your understanding of biblical faith.

Crosswalk www.crosswalk.com

Crosswalk provides a variety of resources, including articles, devotionals, and videos, to help Christians grow in their faith and understand their relationship with God.

Bible Study Tools www.biblestudytools.com

This site offers extensive resources for Bible study, including articles, commentaries, and study guides that can aid in understanding and growing your faith in God.

Relevant Magazine www.relevantmagazine.com

Relevant Magazine covers contemporary Christian issues and provides articles that challenge and inspire believers to live out their faith authentically.

These resources will support and enhance your journey of strengthening your relationship with God through faith. Whether through books, articles, or online resources, you'll find a wealth of knowledge and inspiration to help you grow in your faith and live out your God given purpose.

ABOUT THE AUTHOR

Hello, I'm Eric G Reid, Co-Founder and Editor-in-Chief at Skinny Brown Dog Media. My passion lies in guiding authors and leaders like you to discover and share your unique stories and identities. With over a decade of experience in digital media and publishing, I am committed to helping others find their true voice and purpose through the art of storytelling.

My journey in publishing started with a desire to help others share their stories. As an author myself, I know the joy and challenges of bringing words to life on the page. Over the years, I've worked with a diverse array of authors, speakers, and coaches, each bringing their own unique voice and message. This experience has underscored for me the transformative power of words and the importance of authenticity in our stories.

My faith is a cornerstone of my life and work. I firmly believe that understanding our identity in Christ is essential to living a life of purpose and fulfillment. This conviction fuels my dedication to helping others discover and embrace their God given identities.. Feel free to reach out to me at Eric@SkinnyBrownDogMedia.com.

I look forward to supporting you on your journey of self-discovery and storytelling.

ABOUT THE WHOLE LIFE DEVOTIONAL SERIES

Welcome to the Whole Life Devotional Series. Think of it as a spiritual road trip through different parts of your faith journey. Each book is like a friendly guide, helping you explore God's love, beef up your faith, and figure out how to live a life that really matters.

I am not about fancy theological jargon here. Instead, I am an authentic voice and practical insights, biblical wisdom, and real-life stories that'll help you grow closer to God. The series is intended to feel like you are a chat with a good friend who just happens to be pretty passionate about personal growth and faith stuff.

Feel free to drop me a line at Eric@SkinnyBrownDogMedia.com. I'd love to hear from you as we dive into this adventure of figuring out who God made us to be. Let's grow together!

Books in the Series:

Identity: Discovering Who You Are

- Focus: Understanding and embracing your identity in Christ.
- Themes: Self-worth, God's love, being made in God's image.
- Summary: Discover your true identity in Christ and replace the world's misconceptions with the solid truth of God's Word.

Faith: Strengthening Your Relationship with God

- Focus: Deepening your faith and spiritual growth.
- Themes: Prayer, Bible study, spiritual disciplines.
- Summary: Cultivate a vibrant, everyday faith that transforms your life in tangible ways.

Transformation: Embracing Spiritual Growth

- Focus: Becoming more Christlike through spiritual growth.
- Themes: Sanctification, growth in virtues, spiritual maturity.
- Summary: Embrace the process of spiritual transformation and grow deeper in your relationship with God.

Wisdom: Making Godly Decisions

- Focus: Making wise, biblically based decisions.
- Themes: Discernment, moral choices, God's guidance.
- Summary: Learn to make wise decisions that align with God's will and seek His divine guidance.

Surrender: Embracing God's Will

- Focus: Surrendering to God's will.
- Themes: Trust, obedience, letting go, faith.
- Summary: Understand and practice the concept of surrender, letting go of your own plans, and embracing God's perfect will.

Peace: Finding Rest in a Busy World

- Focus: Finding true rest and peace in God.
- Themes: Stress management, trust in God, spiritual rest.
- Summary: Find peace and rest through trust in God and learn practical steps to manage stress and embrace spiritual rest.

Additional books in the series are currently under consideration by the publisher. Please follow for updates and announcements on upcoming releases. Stay connected and be the first to know about new titles and insights designed to deepen your spiritual journey.

I AM

A CHILD OF GOD THROUGH FAITH:
"So, in Christ Jesus you are all children of God through faith."
—Galatians 3:26

JUSTIFIED BY FAITH:
"Therefore, since we have been justified through faith,
we have peace with God through our Lord Jesus Christ."
—Romans 5:1

LIVING BY FAITH:
"For we live by faith, not by sight."
—2 Corinthians 5:7

STRENGTHENED IN FAITH:
"I pray that out of his glorious riches he may strengthen you with
power through his Spirit in your inner being, so that Christ
may dwell in your hearts through faith."
—Ephesians 3:1617

SAVED BY GRACE THROUGH FAITH:
"For it is by grace you have been saved, through faith—and
this is not from yourselves, it is the gift of God."
—Ephesians 2:8

HOLDING FIRM TO FAITH:
"Let us hold unswervingly to the hope we profess,
for he who promised is faithful."
—Hebrews 10:23

WALKING IN THE LIGHT:
"But if we walk in the light, as he is in the light,
we have fellowship with one another, and the blood of Jesus,
his Son, purifies us from all sin."
—1 John 1:7

OVERCOMING THE WORLD THROUGH FAITH:
"For everyone born of God overcomes the world.
This is the victory that has overcome the world, even our faith."
—1 John 5:4

SHIELDED BY FAITH:
"Who through faith are shielded by God's power until the coming of the
salvation that is ready to be revealed in the last time."
—1 Peter 1:5

CONFIDENT IN HOPE:
"Now faith is confidence in what we hope for and
assurance about what we do not see."
—Hebrews 11:1

A WITNESS TO GOD'S FAITHFULNESS:
"I will sing of the Lord's great love forever; with my mouth I will make your
faithfulness known through all generations."
—Psalm 89:1

AN HEIR TO THE PROMISES OF GOD:
"Therefore, the promise comes by faith, so that it may be by grace
and may be guaranteed to all Abraham's offspring—not only to those who
are of the law but also to those who have the faith of Abraham.
He is the father of us all."
—Romans 4:16

LIVING A LIFE THAT PLEASES GOD:
"And without faith it is impossible to please God,
because anyone who comes to him must believe that he exists
and that he rewards those who earnestly seek him."
—Hebrews 11:6

TRUSTING IN GOD'S PLAN:
"'For I know the plans I have for you,' declares the Lord, 'plans to prosper
you and not to harm you, plans to give you hope and a future.'"
—Jeremiah 29:11

FILLED WITH JOY AND PEACE THROUGH FAITH:
"May the God of hope fill you with all joy and peace as you trust in him,
so that you may overflow with hope by the power of the Holy Spirit."
—Romans 15:13

ROOTED AND ESTABLISHED IN LOVE THROUGH FAITH:
"So that Christ may dwell in your hearts through faith.
And I pray that you, being rooted and established in love."
—Ephesians 3:17